Hello, I'm a bossy hand.

Do what I say and you'll ...

WIN POINTS!

Say these words if you want to

LOSE POINTS!

Are we there yet?

I'm bored.

It's not fair.

Lose 100 points

Okay, lets start with some car games!

Put the initials of each winner in the provided boxes. You can add up the score later. Some games have more than one box, this means you can play the game more than once.

The winners initials!

Spot a cat
30 points.

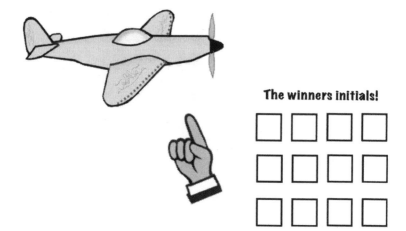

Spot an Airplane.

60 points

Spot a grumpy driver.

45 points

The winners initials!

Spot a happy driver.

80 points

The winners initials!

Spot a singing driver.

150 points

The winners initials!

Someone who looks a bit like a Pirate
70 points

The winners initials!

Spot a motorcyclist.
90 points

A grumpy driver with BIG hair.

150 points

A happy driver wearing spectacles.

100 points

The winners initials!

A driver in shades,
who thinks he's cool.

160 points

FILL IN THE BLANKS!

Sitting in this car is better than

The winners initials!

Example:

Than being stuck in the jungle
eating putrid parrot pancakes!

Best answer wins

40 points

My Mum is so kind because...

Example:

She bakes me a cake, when I'm sad.

Best answer wins

75 points

My Dad is great because...

Example:

because he tells funny jokes.

Best answer wins

75 points

X-ray Test

Kleptomania patient's X-ray!

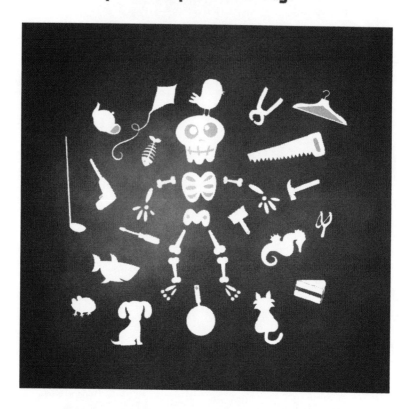

Get a pen and a piece of paper, you have 5
minutes to try and remember every item
collected by the patient. The answers on the
next page 70 points for every item noted.

X-ray Test

Test Results

Dog	Teapot
Frog	Kite
Shark	Bird
Screwdriver	Pliers
Golf club	Coat hanger
Drill	Saw
Fish	Hammer
Cat	Seahorse
Saucepan	Catapult
	Cake

Tick objects remembered!

The winners initials!

☐ ☐ ☐ ☐
☐ ☐ ☐ ☐
☐ ☐ ☐ ☐

The winners initials!

☐ ☐ ☐ ☐
☐ ☐ ☐ ☐
☐ ☐ ☐ ☐

Tests Dad's Brain!

```
D C R E F J L S S I E N D D P
A U B O J M Y D T I X N X M E
U F L V T R E L N M D W I P T
J J R V I C A D E G R Y S L V
S A C N Y T O M I M O D I A W
V G G L I S C D T C L R T S E
E E U P K R N C A Z I Z R T S
S F S O Z Q L O P W K N P E R
D O C S W C J Q I D P E E R U
H S K E L E T O N T U F W S N
Y Z L A C I D E M Q C Z X J Q
O L D Q E F F L R Y M E J Y I
N O I T P I R C S E R P J A Y
W B T I L J C V J M I Q Q N R
R W P K Z S A P O D Q G E N I
```

Dad has 30 minutes to find the hidden words!

Doctor   Nurse

Hospital   Patients

Injections   Plasters

Medical   Prescription

Medicine   Skeleton

Dad's a genius if he also finds the one extra word not listed!

1 Minute to find the C.

The winners initials!

The winners initials!

Draw funny drivers, every funny face wins 400 points.

The winners initials!

Bats
How many?

700 points
How many bats and how many
sausages can you find?
2 mins only to guess!

Sausages
How many?

The winners initials!

Answer: Bats= 67
Sausages = 84

FILL IN THESE BLANKS!

The winners initials!

My favourite singer is ....
The best movie ever is...
The worst song ever is...
Vacations are great because...
I love traveling because...
My favourite sportsman is...
If I ruled the world I'd...
If I was president I wouldn't...
Each best answer wins
50 points!

TONGUE TWISTER
TIME!

Turn this page using your tongue?
for 100 points, if the page remains dry!

TONGUE Twisters
If you can repeat, you win

The winners initials!

CAN YOU CAN A CAN
AS A CANNER CAN
CAN A CAN?

150 points

TONGUE Twisters

How many **boards**
Could the Mongols
hoard
If the Mongol hordes
got **bored**?

The winners initials!

80 points

ONGUE Twisters

Denise sees the
FLEECE,
Denise sees the
FLEAS.
At least Denise could
SNEEZE
and feed and FREEZE
the FLEAS.

The winners initials!

120 points

ONGUE Twisters

Roberta ran rings around
the Roman ruins.

The winners initials!

50 points

TONGUE Twisters

I WISH TO WISH THE WISH YOU WISH TO WISH, BUT IF YOU WISH THE WISH THE WITCH WISHES, I WON'T WISH THE WISH YOU WISH TO WISH.

The winners initials!

150 points

TONGUE Twisters

tHERE WAS A FISHERMAN NAMED FISHER
WHO FISHED FOR SOME FISH IN A FISSURE.
till A FISH WITH A GRIN,
pulled THE FISHERMAN IN
now THEY'RE FISHING tHE FISSURE FOR FISHER.

The winners initials!

170 points

FILL IN THESE BLANKS!

My favourite singer is ....
The best movie ever is...
The worst song ever is...
Vacations are great because...
I love traveling because...
My favourite sportsman is...
If I ruled the world I'd...
If I was president I wouldn't...
Each best answer wins
50 points!

The winners initials!

☐	☐	☐	☐
☐	☐	☐	☐
☐	☐	☐	☐

The winners initials!

☐	☐	☐	☐
☐	☐	☐	☐
☐	☐	☐	☐

LIMERICK TIME!

I once new a man called O'Delli
Who's brain constituted just jelly
He thru wobblers all day
For his mind would sway
As unstable as his belly

Write New Limericks!
FOR BIG POINTS!

Turn the page using just your
nose, you're about to write prose.

I once knew a man from O,Lea
200 points □

I once knew a girl called Sue
250 points □

RIDDLE TIME!
Choose team Mum
or team Dad!

DAD
vs
MUM

What do the numbers
11, 69, and 88 all have
in common?

Answer: They read the
same backwards and
forward.

The winners initials!

150 points

RIDDLE TIME!
Dad vs Mum

WHICH ANIMAL EATS
WITH ITS EARS?

ANSWER: ALL OF
THEM SINCE NO
ANIMAL TAKE OFF ITS
EARS TO EAT!

The winners initials!

150 points

Dad vs Mum

A DONKEY WAS TIED TO A
ROPE SIX FEET LONG. A BALE
OF HAY WAS 18 FEET AWAY
AND THE DONKEY WANTED
TO EAT THE HAY. HOW
COULD HE DO IT?

ANSWER: VERY EASILY AS
THE ROPE WASNT TIED TO
ANYTHING.

The winners initials!

150 points

RIDDLE TIME!

Dad vs Mum

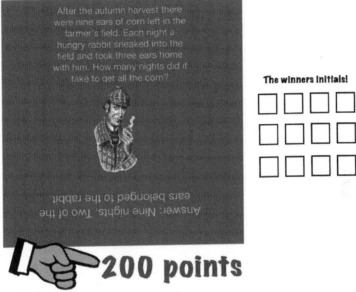

After the autumn harvest there were nine ears of corn left in the farmer's field. Each night a hungry rabbit sneaked into the field and took three ears home with him. How many nights did it take to get all the corn?

Answer: Nine nights. Two of the ears belonged to the rabbit.

The winners initials!

⬜ ⬜ ⬜ ⬜
⬜ ⬜ ⬜ ⬜
⬜ ⬜ ⬜ ⬜

200 points

Without a bridle or a saddle,

across a thing I ride and straddle,

And those I ride, by the help of me,

though almost blind are made to see. What am I?

Answer: Eye glasses

The winners initials!

⬜ ⬜ ⬜ ⬜
⬜ ⬜ ⬜ ⬜
⬜ ⬜ ⬜ ⬜

200 points

Poor Dad!

Let's sing him a song, to cheer him up!

Anyone who sings wins
300 points

Anyone who breaks a window loses
300 points

Before you start singing turn this page over using just your big toe.

200 points!

The winners initials!

This Old Man!

This old man, he played one
He played knick-knack on my thumb
With a knick-knack patty-whack, give a dog a bone
This old man came rolling home

This old man, he played two
He played knick-knack on my shoe
With a knick-knack patty-whack, give a dog a bone
This old man came rolling home

This old man, he played three
He played knick-knack on my knee
With a knick-knack patty-whack, give a dog a bone
This old man came rolling home

This old man, he played four
He played knick-knack on my door
With a knick-knack patty-whack, give a dog a bone
This old man came rolling home

This old man, he played five
He played knick-knack on my hive
With a knick-knack patty-whack, give a dog a bone
This old man came rolling home

This old man, he played six
He played knick-knack on my sticks
With a knick-knack patty-whack, give a dog a bone
This old man came rolling home

This old man, he played seven
He played knick-knack up in heaven
With a knick-knack patty-whack, give a dog a bone
This old man came rolling home

This Old Man!

This old man, he played eight
He played knick-knack on my gate
With a knick-knack patty-whack, give a dog a bone
This old man came rolling home

This old man, he played nine
He played knick-knack on my spine
With a knick-knack patty-whack, give a dog a bone
This old man came rolling home

This old man, he played ten
He played knick-knack once ag'n
With a knick-knack patty-whack, give a dog a bone
This old man came rolling home

Well Done!

300 points

Extra points if you sing the next song
in a SILLY voice!

The winners initials!

☐	☐	☐	☐
☐	☐	☐	☐
☐	☐	☐	☐

Round and round the cobbler's bench
The monkey chased the weasel,
The monkey thought 'twas all in fun
Pop! Goes the weasel.

A penny for a spool of thread
A penny for a needle,
That's the way the money goes,
Pop! Goes the weasel.

A half a pound of tupenny rice,
A half a pound of treacle.
Mix it up and make it nice,
Pop! Goes the weasel.

Up and down the London road,
In and out of the Eagle,
That's the way the money goes,
Pop! Goes the weasel.

I've no time to plead and pine,
I've no time to wheedle,
Kiss me quick and then I'm gone
Pop! Goes the weasel.

150 points

400 extra for SILLY voice!

The winners initials!

Now sing any song you like!

Whoever sings the best

WINS!

400 points

The winners initials!

☐ ☐ ☐ ☐
☐ ☐ ☐ ☐
☐ ☐ ☐ ☐

LETS HAND JIVE!
(CAR DANCING)

THIS IS HOW DAD DANCED
WHEN HE WAS YOUNG!

1) Pat your thighs twice.

2) Clap twice.

3) Wave your hands, one over the front of your chest. Then do it with the other hand on top.

4) Bump your fists twice, one on top of the Then do it with the other fist on top.

5) Point your right thumb over your right shoulder twice, then your left thumb over your left shoulder twice. Play this song and put it all together to the beat! Pat-pat-clap-clap-hand-hand-bump-bump thumb-thumb!

500 points

The winners initials!

☐ ☐ ☐ ☐

☐ ☐ ☐ ☐

☐ ☐ ☐ ☐

Have you got a pencil, because you'll need
one for the next page!

Drawing Fun!

Draw whoever is sitting next
to you, vote to decided who created
the best drawing!

1

2

3

4

Best drawing wins □
500 points!

Drawing Fun!

**Whoever capture moms
beauty wins this time!**

1

2

3

4

Best drawing wins ☐
500 points! 👉

Drawing Fun!

Okay now draw whatever
you like!

1

2

3

4

Best drawing wins □
500 points!

Let's play the shopping list game.

The Rules

To begin, the first player names an object available at a grocery store that starts with the letter A. The next player has to repeat what the first player said and then add another grocery item that starts with a B. For example, if player one says "artichokes," player two would repeat "artichokes" and then might add "broccoli." If you forget even one item you're our out.

The player with the greatest memory wins!

700 points

The winners initials!

☐	☐	☐	☐
☐	☐	☐	☐
☐	☐	☐	☐

The winners initials!

☐	☐	☐	☐
☐	☐	☐	☐
☐	☐	☐	☐

FORTUNATELY UNFORTUNATELY

The Rules

In this game, one person will make an unfortunate statement, and then another player will counter the statement with a positive fortunately response.

"Unfortunately I was bitten by a crocodile".

"Fortunately it was only 3 inches long".

Each Participant Wins!

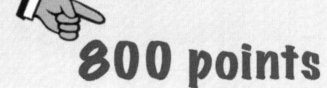

800 points

The winners initials!

☐ ☐ ☐ ☐

☐ ☐ ☐ ☐

☐ ☐ ☐ ☐

The winners initials!

☐ ☐ ☐ ☐

☐ ☐ ☐ ☐

☐ ☐ ☐ ☐

Okay let's cheer up dad with some jokes!

Take turns to tell the jokes on the next pages everyone who tells a joke wins!

20 points for every joke told!

The winners initials!

The winners initials!

The winners initials!

The winners initials!

The winners initials!

The winners initials!

The winners initials!

The winners initials!

LETS TELL JOKES!

Q: What goes up and down but does not move?
A: Stairs

Q: Where should a 500 pound alien go?
A: On a diet

Q: What did one toilet say to the other?
A: You look a bit flushed.

Q: Why did the picture go to jail?
A: Because it was framed.

Q: What did one wall say to the other wall?
A: I'll meet you at the corner.

Q: What did the paper say to the pencil?
A: Write on!

Q: What do you call a boy named Lee that no one talks to?
A: Lonely

Q: What gets wetter the more it dries?
A: A towel.

Q: Why do bicycles fall over?
A: Because they are two-tired!

Q: Why do dragons sleep during the day?
A: So they can fight knights!

LETS TELL JOKES!

Q: What did one elevator say to the other elevator?
A: I think I'm coming down with something!

Q: Why was the belt arrested?
A: Because it held up some pants!

Q: Why was everyone so tired on April 1st?
A: They had just finished a March of 31 days.

Q: Which hand is it better to write with?
A: Neither, it's best to write with a pen!

Q: Why can't your nose be 12 inches long?
A: Because then it would be a foot!

Q: What makes the calendar seem so popular?
A: Because it has a lot of dates!

Q: Why did Mickey Mouse take a trip into space?
A: He wanted to find Pluto!

Q: What is green and has yellow wheels?
A: Grass.....I lied about the wheels!

Q: Did you hear about the robbery last night?
A: Two clothes pins held up a pair of pants!

Q: Why do you go to bed every night?
A: Because the bed won't come to you!

LETS TELL JOKES!

Q: What do you call a sleeping bull?
A: A bull-dozer.

Q: How do you fit more pigs on your farm?
A: Build a sty-scraper!

Q: What did the farmer call the cow that had no milk?
A: An udder failure.

Q: Why do gorillas have big nostrils?
A: Because they have big fingers!

Q: What do you get from a pampered cow?
A: Spoiled milk.

Q: Why are teddy bears never hungry?
A: They are always stuffed!

Q: Why do fish live in salt water?
A: Because pepper makes them sneeze!

Q: What do you get from a pampered cow?
A: Spoiled milk.

Q: Where do polar bears vote?
A: The North Poll

Q: What did the judge say when the skunk walked in the court room?
A: Odor in the Court.

LETS TELL JOKES!

Q: What sound do porcupines make when they kiss?
A: Ouch!

Q: Why did the snake cross the road?
A: To get to the other ssssssside!

Q: Why are fish so smart?
A: Because they live in schools.

Q: What do you call a cow that won't give milk?
A: A milk dud!

Q: When is a well dressed lion like a weed?
A: When he's a dandelion (dandy lion)

Q: How does a lion greet the other animals in the field?
A: Pleased to eat you.

Q: What happened when the lion ate the comedian?
A: He felt funny!

Q: What fish only swims at night?
A: A starfish!

Q: Why is a fish easy to weigh?
A: Because it has its own scales!

Q: Why did the lion spit out the clown?
A: Because he tasted funny!

LETS TELL JOKES!

Q: How did the music teacher get locked in the classroom?
A: His keys were inside the piano!

Q: What do elves learn in school?
A: The elf-abet!

Q: What did you learn in school today?
A: Not enough, I have to go back tomorrow!

Q: What holds the sun up in the sky?
A: Sunbeams!

Q: What object is king of the classroom?
A: The ruler!

Q: When do astronauts eat?
A: At launch time!

Q: What did the pencil sharpener say to the pencil?
A: Stop going in circles and get to the point!

Q: How does the barber cut the moon's hair?
A: E-clipse it!

Q: What happened when the wheel was invented?
A: It caused a revolution!

Q: What do librarians take with them when they go fishing?
A: Bookworms

LETS TELL JOKES!

Q: What did Cinderella say when her photos did not show up?
A: Someday my prints will come!

Q: Why was the broom late?
A: It over swept!

Q: What part of the car is the laziest?
A: The wheels, because they are always tired!

Q: What did the stamp say to the envelope?
A: Stick with me and we will go places!

Q: What is blue and goes ding dong?
A: An Avon lady at the North Pole!

Q: We're you long in the hospital?
A: No, I was the same size I am now!

Q: Why couldn't the pirate play cards?
A: Because he was sitting on the deck!

Q: What did the laundryman say to the impatient customer?
A: Keep your shirt on!

Q: What's the difference between a TV and a newspaper?
A: Ever tried swatting a fly with a TV?

Poor Dad, he's heard enough jokes!
He wants to hear his children sing!

Everyone Sing For Dad!

Lyrics

For he's a jolly good fellow,
For he's a jolly good fellow,
For he's a jolly good fellow,
Which nobody can deny.

Which nobody can deny,
Which nobody can deny.
For he's a jolly good fellow,
Which nobody can deny.

Dads gone all shy!

When the saints go marching in

Oh when the saints
Go marching in
Oh when the saints go marching in
Oh I want to be in that number
When the saints go marching in

Oh when the band
Begins to play
Oh when the band begins to play
Oh I want to be in that number
When the band begins to play

Oh when the kids
Begin to dance
Oh when the kids begin to dance
Oh I want to be in that number
When the kids begin to dance
One, two, three, four, five, six, seven

Oh when the saints
Go marching in
Oh when the saints go marching in
Oh I want to be in that number
When the saints go marching in
Oh I want to be in that number
When the saints
Go marching in

Sing For 200 points

The winners initials!

The winners initials!

LET PLAY HUG BUG!

HUG BUG

The Rules

Every player who spots a Volkswagen, gets a hug from Mum and **400** points.
Every player who spots an older model, gets a hug and **600 points**.

The winners initials!

☐ ☐ ☐ ☐

☐ ☐ ☐ ☐

☐ ☐ ☐ ☐

The winners initials!

☐ ☐ ☐ ☐

☐ ☐ ☐ ☐

☐ ☐ ☐ ☐

Spot the old women and the young lady.

250 points

The winners initials!

☐	☐	☐	☐
☐	☐	☐	☐
☐	☐	☐	☐

The winners initials!

☐	☐	☐	☐
☐	☐	☐	☐
☐	☐	☐	☐

Spot the two faces and the vase.

250 points

Spot the Indian and the Eskimo cave.

250 points

The winners initials!

The winners initials!

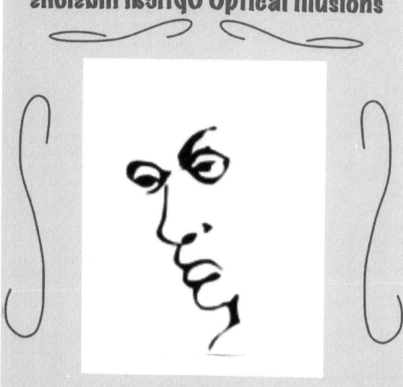

Spot the face and the word liar.

250 points

The winners initials!

□ □ □ □
□ □ □ □
□ □ □ □

The winners initials!

□ □ □ □
□ □ □ □
□ □ □ □

Spot the Elephant leg illusion.

250 points

The winners initials!

☐ ☐ ☐ ☐
☐ ☐ ☐ ☐
☐ ☐ ☐ ☐

The winners initials!

☐ ☐ ☐ ☐
☐ ☐ ☐ ☐
☐ ☐ ☐ ☐

snoisulli lsoitqO Optical illusions

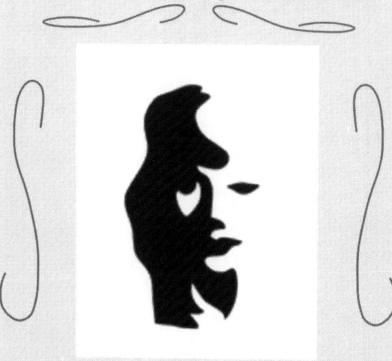

Spot the man with the horn and the woman's face.

250 points

The winners initials!

☐ ☐ ☐ ☐
☐ ☐ ☐ ☐
☐ ☐ ☐ ☐

The winners initials!

☐ ☐ ☐ ☐
☐ ☐ ☐ ☐
☐ ☐ ☐ ☐

snoisulli lacitpO Optical illusions

Spot the face and the land.

250 points

Let's Play 20 Questions!

20 Questions
Object: To figure out the mystery item by asking Yes/No questions.

How to Play:
One person thinks of a 'mystery item', and gives the general category, such as:
Famous Person
Famous Place
Famous Thing
The rest of the group asks Yes/No questions until someone guesses the 'mystery item'. The person who guesses the item gets to think of the next item.

The winners get **400 points**

The winners initials!

☐ ☐ ☐ ☐
☐ ☐ ☐ ☐
☐ ☐ ☐ ☐

The winners initials!

☐ ☐ ☐ ☐
☐ ☐ ☐ ☐
☐ ☐ ☐ ☐

LETS PLAY!
Rock Paper Scissors

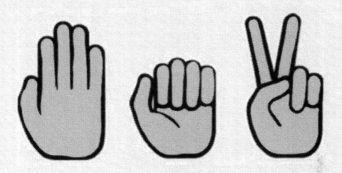

Rock Paper Scissors: Four Simple Rules
Rock crushes scissors.
Scissors cut paper.
Paper smothers rock.

PLAY GENTLY AND WIN

500 POINTS!

The winners initials!

☐ ☐ ☐ ☐
☐ ☐ ☐ ☐
☐ ☐ ☐ ☐

The winners initials!

☐ ☐ ☐ ☐
☐ ☐ ☐ ☐
☐ ☐ ☐ ☐

What's hidden in the picture?

300 points

The winners initials!

The winners initials!

What's hidden in the picture?

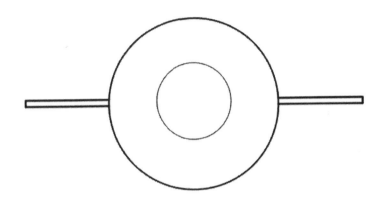

300 points

The winners initials!

The winners initials!

What's hidden in the picture?

300 points

Answer
A worm that crossed a razor blade.

The winners initials!

The winners initials!

What's hidden in the picture?

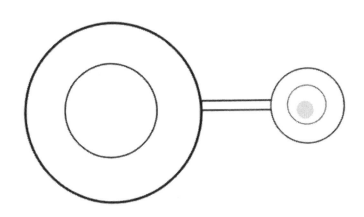

300 points

The winners initials!

☐ ☐ ☐ ☐
☐ ☐ ☐ ☐
☐ ☐ ☐ ☐

The winners initials!

☐ ☐ ☐ ☐
☐ ☐ ☐ ☐
☐ ☐ ☐ ☐

What's hidden in the picture?

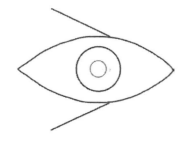 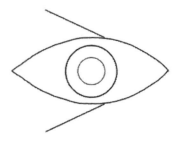

300 points

The winners initials!

☐ ☐ ☐ ☐
☐ ☐ ☐ ☐
☐ ☐ ☐ ☐

The winners initials!

☐ ☐ ☐ ☐
☐ ☐ ☐ ☐
☐ ☐ ☐ ☐

What's hidden in the picture?

300 points

The winners initials!

The winners initials!

What's hidden in the picture?

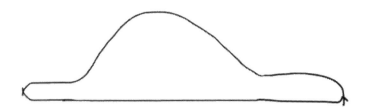

300 points

Answer
After the python met the zookeeper.

The winners initials!

☐ ☐ ☐ ☐
☐ ☐ ☐ ☐
☐ ☐ ☐ ☐

The winners initials!

☐ ☐ ☐ ☐
☐ ☐ ☐ ☐
☐ ☐ ☐ ☐

Copy this picture in only 2 mins!

How do you make a jelly baby laugh?

Tickle it's jelly button.

1

2

3

4

5

Have a vote on who's drawing is closest.

The winners initials!

☐	☐	☐	☐
☐	☐	☐	☐
☐	☐	☐	☐

500 points

Copy this picture in only 2 mins!

What kind of photos does a turtle take?

Shell-fies.

1

2

3

4

5

Have a vote on who's drawing is closest.

The winners initials!

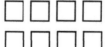

500 points

Copy this picture in only **2 mins!**

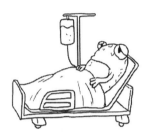

How does a frog with broken legs feel?

Very un-hoppy.

1

2

3

4

5

Have a vote on who's drawing is closest.

The winners initials!

☐	☐	☐	☐
☐	☐	☐	☐
☐	☐	☐	☐

500 points

Copy this picture in only 2 mins!

What do you give a sick bird?

Tweet-ment.

1

2

3

4

5

Have a vote on who's drawing is closest.

The winners initials!

500 points

Copy this picture in only 2 mins!

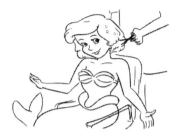

How do mermaids like
their hair cut?

Short and pearly.

1

2

3

4

5

Have a vote on
who's drawing is
closest.

The winners initials!

☐ ☐ ☐ ☐
☐ ☐ ☐ ☐
☐ ☐ ☐ ☐

500 points

Copy this picture in only 5 mins!
Blindfolded.

What did one volcano say to the other volcano?

I lava you.

1

2

3

4

5

Have a vote on who's drawing is closest.

The winners initials!

500 points

Copy this picture in only 5 mins!
Blindfolded.

How do mermaids get to balls?

By taxi crab.

1

2

3

4

5

Have a vote on who's drawing is closest.

The winners initials!

500 points

Copy this picture in only 5 mins!
Blindfolded.

Why was the small strawberry crying?

Because his parents were in a bit of a jam.

1

2

3

4

5

Have a vote on who's drawing is closest.

The winners initials!

☐ ☐ ☐ ☐
☐ ☐ ☐ ☐
☐ ☐ ☐ ☐

500 points

Take turns one min each to
find words that describe Disney films.

B	A	M	P	O	C	A	H	O	N	T	A	S	K
A	B	U	A	S	A	E	E	W	I	F	P	B	O
E	N	C	B	T	R	L	A	T	N	L	A	I	O
N	T	Z	A	C	S	L	O	R	M	M	S	G	B
T	S	A	U	S	L	Y	A	R	D	N	C	S	E
P	O	L	U	E	S	L	C	B	A	M	B	I	L
Y	E	B	R	T	A	O	B	B	O	S	O	E	G
S	I	I	O	D	B	U	N	A	Z	R	A	T	N
R	M	R	D	M	N	A	P	R	E	T	E	P	U
E	Y	I	U	B	L	O	A	B	O	L	T	M	J
T	N	D	U	B	F	A	N	T	A	S	I	A	S
R	O	B	I	N	H	O	O	D	M	U	L	A	N
D	T	M	O	N	S	T	E	R	S	I	N	C	N
L	U	U	T	Y	T	Y	U	N	T	C	E	A	N

ALADDIN
MULAN
WALL-E
MONSTERS INC
CARS
TOY STORY
JUNGLE BOOK
FANTASIA
DUMBO
BAMBI
PETER PAN
HERCULES
TARZAN
BOLT
POCAHONTAS
ROBIN HOOD

The winner!

1000 points

Find the hidden words
no clues given, 3 mins each,
whoever find most words wins.

R	R	B	A	L	L	M	P	V	R	N	T	E	U
U	O	R	A	B	V	O	I	R	O	N	P	E	P
E	O	C	N	Y	L	L	O	L	E	X	T	R	A
E	C	P	E	P	X	E	B	F	E	L	O	P	L
H	T	L	B	E	E	O	C	C	E	G	E	O	O
L	P	O	P	L	N	L	A	H	L	E	L	E	L
U	E	V	C	G	N	E	B	E	T	V	P	N	E
R	X	E	O	L	P	R	L	M	C	I	E	N	V
O	O	L	E	E	O	L	O	P	U	N	A	E	L
O	E	P	C	R	E	G	T	S	C	R	I	F	B
S	O	I	E	N	A	B	S	U	F	B	C	R	C
H	T	E	E	P	E	E	H	E	U	L	G	N	P
T	A	P	L	R	M	U	L	P	O	E	P	M	L
E	A	O	U	E	L	P	F	N	O	A	C	M	P

The winner!

1000 points

Take turns one min each to find words that describe mom!

I	L	U	Y	U	O	U	R	E	C	N	A	D	D
A	P	R	E	T	T	Y	E	L	L	E	P	A	U
S	A	T	H	O	U	G	H	T	F	U	L	K	O
Q	U	W	F	T	S	T	N	U	L	T	N	D	T
U	U	E	G	N	I	G	Q	N	D	C	Y	N	P
I	D	T	G	N	N	I	Y	K	D	N	E	E	A
R	C	G	E	E	G	N	I	L	A	N	G	U	T
K	L	Q	G	I	E	G	T	M	D	G	I	E	I
Y	C	E	E	I	R	F	I	N	E	D	C	K	E
T	N	R	N	I	E	C	L	N	P	D	U	P	N
M	I	C	T	I	C	E	G	T	A	E	R	C	C
E	I	R	L	E	I	N	T	T	E	E	W	S	E
I	N	T	E	L	L	I	G	E	N	T	T	T	E
H	I	R	D	A	T	E	Y	L	I	A	I	C	S

PRETTY
KIND
QUIRKY
SINGER
SWEET
GENTLE
INTELLIGENT
DANCER
THOUGHTFUL
PATIENCE
DYNAMIC
CUDDLY

The winner!

1000 points

Take turns one min each to find words that describe dad.

I	W	L	H	I	L	A	R	I	O	U	S	I	K
D	I	E	H	E	Y	T	N	E	I	T	A	P	N
E	T	A	A	I	I	N	H	N	I	E	S	I	W
I	T	T	N	C	N	L	N	G	N	D	N	I	K
G	Y	U	D	S	T	D	T	U	D	L	T	A	C
G	U	G	S	Y	E	N	S	G	F	C	G	I	H
N	O	S	O	T	L	O	L	N	F	M	A	W	A
O	I	I	M	N	L	N	K	N	L	O	N	L	R
R	Y	S	E	M	I	M	S	T	R	D	A	N	M
T	H	I	S	T	G	C	L	S	E	E	T	S	I
S	Y	L	I	N	E	I	E	H	H	O	S	S	N
G	O	U	A	L	N	T	U	Y	O	I	T	A	G
Y	R	M	O	M	T	M	Y	E	M	O	A	S	U
O	G	K	I	N	E	H	G	A	I	I	A	I	I

FUNNY
STRONG
HANDSOME
INTELLIGENT
HILARIOUS
CALM
PATIENT
WITTY
SHY
WISE
CHARMING
KIND

The winner!

1000 points

Take turns one min each to
find words that describe vacation fun.

A	I	H	U	R	L	L	G	N	I	R	A	H	S
I	F	A	M	I	L	Y	R	N	M	I	L	A	N
I	C	N	N	E	W	F	R	I	E	N	D	S	B
C	C	E	L	E	I	A	I	Y	N	G	A	S	R
N	B	L	L	L	E	S	E	E	A	D	S	D	T
G	E	F	A	O	A	N	C	V	A	I	H	L	H
N	A	R	L	H	L	U	V	O	R	N	A	A	A
I	C	E	D	A	J	L	G	L	N	I	F	I	N
C	H	A	L	O	A	R	I	H	N	N	L	H	K
N	E	K	Y	W	O	A	A	E	T	G	O	N	F
A	C	N	D	C	I	E	L	A	S	E	H	A	U
D	M	A	E	R	C	E	C	I	O	A	R	F	L
W	I	G	I	G	I	J	E	A	N	A	A	A	A
L	V	R	L	I	M	A	N	C	E	S	A	I	D

LAUGHTER
FAMILY
LOVE
NEWFRIENDS
SHARING
BEACH
ICE LOLLIES
ICE CREAM
DANCING
DINING
JOY
THANKFUL

The winner!

1000 points

1 story

Name here

Short story competition

Make up a short 2 page story, best story
wins 4000 points. 1000 points to losers.

Page 1

1 story

Name here

Make up a short 2 page story, best story
wins 4000 points. 1000 points to losers.

2 story

Name here

Short story competition

Make up a short 2 page story, best story
wins 4000 points. 1000 points to losers.

Page 1

_____
_____
_____
_____
_____
_____
_____
_____
_____
_____
_____
_____
_____
_____
_____
_____
_____
_____
_____
_____
_____
_____
_____
_____

2 story

Name here

Short story competition

Make up a short 2 page story, best story wins 4000 points. 1000 points to losers.

Page 2

_____
_____
_____
_____
_____
_____
_____
_____
_____
_____
_____
_____
_____
_____
_____
_____
_____
_____
_____
_____
_____
_____
_____
_____

3 story

Name here

Short story competition

Make up a short 2 page story, best story
wins 4000 points. 1000 points to losers.

_____
_____
_____
_____
_____
_____
_____
_____
_____
_____
_____
_____
_____
_____
_____
_____
_____
_____
_____
_____
_____
_____
_____
_____

3 story
Name here

Short story competition

Make up a short 2 page story, best story
wins 4000 points. 1000 points to losers.

Page 2

4 story

Name here

Short story competition

Make up a short 2 page story, best story
wins 4000 points. 1000 points to losers.

Page 1

_____

_____

_____

_____

_____

_____

_____

_____

_____

_____

_____

_____

_____

_____

_____

_____

_____

_____

_____

_____

_____

_____

_____

_____

4 story

Name here

Short story competition

Make up a short 2 page story, best story
wins 4000 points. 1000 points to losers.

Page 2

The winners initials!

Dad Vs Kids!

Q: Imagine you're in a room that is filling with water. There are no windows or doors. How do you get out?
A: Stop imagining!

☐

Q: If you throw a blue stone into the Red Sea, what will it become?
A: Wet.

☐

Q: You can you serve it, but never eat it? What is it?
A: A tennis ball.

☐

Q: Mr. Blue lives in the blue house. Mr. Yellow lives in the yellow house, and Mr. Black lives in the black house. Who lives in the white house?
A: The President.

☐

Q: A girl is sitting in a house at night that has no lights on at all. There is no lamp, no candle, nothing. Yet she is reading. How?
A: The woman is blind, and she is reading Braille.

Q: What has hands but can't clap?
A: A clock.

☐

Q: You draw a line. Without touching it, how do you make the line longer?
A: You draw a shorter line next to it, and it becomes the longer line.

☐

Moms the judge!

Dad vs Kids Coloring Competition!

Dads Side   **Kids Side**

The winner is... ☐

SPY FUN!
YOU ARE ALL NOW SPY'S USE A MIRROR
OR WINDOW REFLECTION TO RECEIVE SECRET ORDERS!

THE FIRST PERSON TO SPOT A TELEPHONE BOX WINS
THE FIRST MISSION! 300 POINTS!

THE FIRST PERSON TO SING THE JAMES BOND THEME
FROM THE SPY WHO LOVED ME WINS 300 POINTS!

SPOT A LORRY THAT'S BEHIND YOU, IF THE DRIVER WAVES
AT YOU IT'S A SPY SIGNAL WIN 600 POINTS!

SPOT AN OLD LADY DRIVING A RED CAR, IF SHE WAVES
AT YOU AND SMILES SHE'S A SPY WIN 700 POINTS!

BE QUITE, SOMEONE HAS PLACED A RECORDING DEVICE
IN YOUR CAR, EVERYONE WHO STAYS ABSOLUTELY QUIET
AND DOESN'T LAUGH, FOR 5 MINUTES WINS 1000 POINTS!

The winners initials!

☐	☐	☐	☐
☐	☐	☐	☐
☐	☐	☐	☐

The winners initials!

☐	☐	☐	☐
☐	☐	☐	☐
☐	☐	☐	☐

Silly book titles you'll have to write your own on the next page!

Remembering Anniversaries
By Betty Wont

Coffee maker
by Phil Turr

Bull Fighting
by Mat Adore

Great Breakfast
By Hammond Deggs

Leaky Boat
By I. C. King

Building Wigwams
By T. P

Long Winter
By Ron. E. Nose

Lovely Breakfast
by Roland Jam

How to keep pigs
By Chris p. Bacon

Life In Prison
By Robbin Banks

Blushing
By Rosie Cheeks

Old School Recording
By Cass Ete

Antibiotics
By Penny Silling

Nosey neighbours
by Annette Curtain

Now create your own!

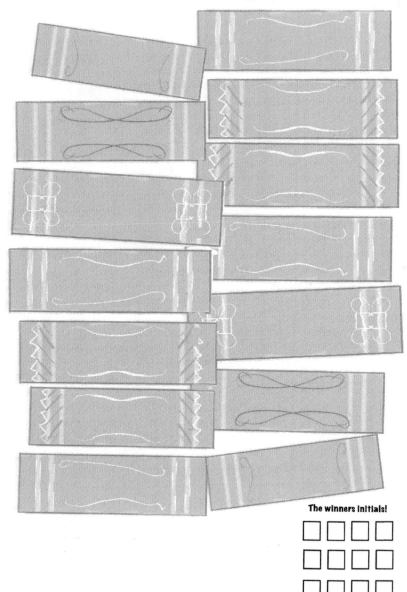

Silly signs, create your own ones on
the next page, best sign wins 2000 points!
All players win 1000 points!

All these signs are real!

Sign outside office:

ATTENTION

THE FIFTH FLOOR
HAS TEMPORARILY
BEEN MOVED TO THE
SEVENTH FLOOR!

Sign outside shop:

Come in
We're
CLOSED

Sign outside a hotel:

FREE WI-FI

STARTING AT
€59 DOLLARS

Sign inside a park:

No signs Allowed!

Sign down a street:

KEEP
← RIGHT

Sign outside flats:

Warning!

Bicycles chained
to these railings
will be moved
without notice
THIS IS A NOTICE!

Create your own!

Sign outside office:

Sign outside shop:

Sign outside a hotel:

Sign inside a park:

Sign down a street:

Sign outside flats:

The winners initials!

The winners initials!

Everyone who write a joke
and signs it wins 1000 points!

The winners initials!

Anyone who can spot six owls can help color in this page!

Once you've found eight lost kittens you can help color in this picture!

Name That Tune!
The rules

Take turns to whistle a tune.

Listeners can take one go each.

If no one names the tune,

The whistler takes the points.

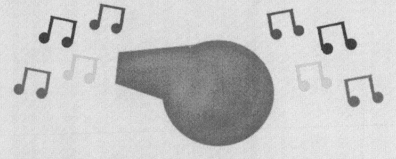

350 points

The winners initials!

☐ ☐ ☐ ☐
☐ ☐ ☐ ☐
☐ ☐ ☐ ☐

The winners initials!

☐ ☐ ☐ ☐
☐ ☐ ☐ ☐
☐ ☐ ☐ ☐

A Balloonatic!

The winners initials!

Doctor sent his silly patient who thought he was a balloon, to a Balloon-atic Asylum but he escaped, please find him!

Balloonatic
Asylum

Write the answers above.

Jump into the jellycopter
and count the what's in the candy
sea, with one eye closed, time two
mins!

Correct answer:
Sweet 15
Candy cane 15
Ice cream 12

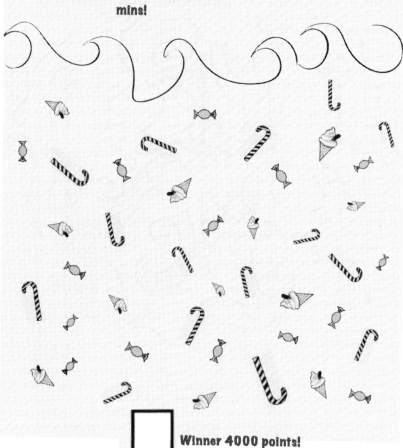

Winner 4000 points!

Whoever scored most points
can draw the face of the naughty
monster!

Write journey details!

Who competed:

Journey:

Time:

Good quality joke books!

With amazing cartoons.

Cindy Merrylove
Ages 6-10

Charlotte Collingwood
Ages 6-12

Cindy Merrylove
Ages 3-5

Mr Krispell
Ages 6-12

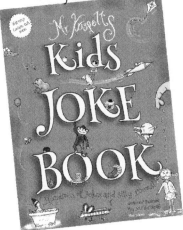

Vacation notes!

New friends

Drawings

A cheerful heart is good medicine. Proverbs 17:22.

Thank you for purchasing my book, if you enjoyed it please give it a review!

Printed in the United States of America

First Printing, 2018

Contact. Sniffitysnoo302@gmail.com

Made in the USA
Middletown, DE
14 June 2023

32546297R00061